Invisible!

By Paul Shipton

Illustrated by Carl Pearce

Activities by Hannah Fish

Contents

OXFORD
UNIVERSITY PRESS

Ben and Rosie are always ready for a new adventure in Grandpa's amazing van.

The van can fly. It can change shape. It can go anywhere in the world in moments … And it can travel through time!

Ben and Rosie are ready for their next adventure. Are *you*?

Grandpa   Ben and Rosie's grandfather, a scientist and inventor

Clunk   Grandpa's robot

Ben   Rosie's brother

Rosie   Ben's sister

Max and his sister Alice   Ben and Rosie's friends

Cooger   a criminal and a very dangerous man

Professor Sparrow   a scientist – he worked with Grandpa years ago and knows about his inventions

Imagine!

Imagine a suit that makes you invisible. What could people use it for? How dangerous would it be? Read *Invisible!* and find out.

Chapter One

The man who walked into the dark room looked around nervously. He pushed his glasses higher up his nose. He was called Sparrow, and he'd never been so frightened in all his life.

Seven or eight people were looking at him. At last one of them spoke: 'Who is this? How can *he* help us?'

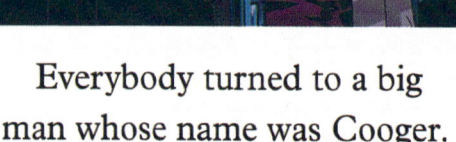

Everybody turned to a big man whose name was Cooger.

Cooger smiled, but the look in his eyes was cold and hard. 'Professor Sparrow is a scientist,' he said quietly. 'And he's going to make us very, *very* rich.'

Cooger turned to the scientist. 'Tell them,' he said.

'Thank you', Sparrow said. He looked around the room. 'Imagine a van that can go anywhere in the world in just moments.'

'What are you talking about?' laughed one of the men.

To answer, Sparrow turned on a computer that was connected to a projector. Everyone sat silently as they watched a video of a van. At first it looked like any other van. But suddenly there were lights all around it … and then it disappeared.

'Where's it gone?' someone asked.

Sparrow gave a little smile. '*Anywhere.*'

Go to page 36 for activities.

Nobody was laughing at Sparrow now. They were beginning to understand: this strange scientist could help them.

'But who could make an amazing van like that?' asked one man.

'Only one person,' answered Sparrow. 'He's the smartest person that I've ever met, and his name is …'

'Grandpa!' shouted Rosie. 'I have some cookies for you!'

She walked into the backyard … and stopped. The yard was empty.

'That's strange!' Rosie said. 'I was sure that Grandpa and Clunk were here.'

'We *are* in the backyard,' said Grandpa's voice.

'Where?' asked Rosie.

Suddenly Grandpa's head appeared – no body, just a head in the air. 'Here,' he said.

Rosie dropped the plate of cookies.

'What's happening?' she asked. 'Where's your body?'

'Don't worry,' Grandpa told her.

Rosie heard a click, and then she could see all of Grandpa. He was wearing a strange yellow suit over his clothes.

Grandpa smiled. 'Clunk and I were just testing my new invention.'

Go to page 37 for activities.

Chapter Two

Inside the house, Grandpa and Clunk told Rosie and Ben about the new invention.

'It's a new kind of material,' Grandpa said. 'This hood goes over your head. Then you push the button on the sleeve. Watch.'

He pushed the button – *Click*! – then disappeared. After a second click, he appeared again.

'Light travels in straight lines,' explained Grandpa. 'But when the suit's on, light travels *around* this material. So the suit – and anybody in it – is invisible.'

'That's amazing, Grandpa,' said Ben. 'But what are you going to use it for?'

'I like watching birds in the backyard. But they usually fly away when they see me.' Grandpa smiled. 'They won't be able to see me now!'

'I have a question,' said Rosie. 'Why did you make the suits bright yellow? It's not very fashionable!'

'Fashion isn't a subject that I know about,' Grandpa laughed. He looked at his watch and stood up. 'Your friends Alice and Max are coming here in ten minutes for a trip in the van. I'll see you both outside. Come on, Clunk. Leave your suit here.'

→ Go to page 38 for activities.

'While we're waiting, please can we try the new suits?' asked Ben.

'Of course,' said Grandpa.

Moments after Grandpa and Clunk left, Rosie and Ben were both wearing the strange yellow suits.

Ben pushed the button and immediately disappeared. 'Can you see me?'

'No!' laughed Rosie.

After they had played with the suits for a few minutes, Rosie pulled down her hood. 'I have a cool idea. Alice and Max are meeting us at the van. Let's turn the suits on and hide in the back of the van. They'll be very surprised!'

Soon they were both in the back of the van.

'Somebody's coming!' whispered Rosie excitedly. 'Get ready, Ben.'

But the person who opened the door wasn't Alice or Max. It was a man that Rosie and Ben had never seen before. A second man got in and started typing on the van's computer.

Rosie wanted to say something – to ask who these men were. But Ben stopped her. He knew that they might be dangerous.

'Let's leave through the back door,' Ben whispered.

There was no time. Suddenly the van started, and then it began to leave. But where was it going?

→ Go to page 39 for activities.

Chapter Three

Professor Sparrow always pushed his glasses higher up his nose when he felt nervous. He did this now as he worked to take the van back to Cooger's building.

Moments later the van appeared in the big garage under the building. Sparrow was surprised, but he tried not to show it. 'That was easy,' he said. 'I thought that there might be a problem.'

He didn't know about Ben and Rosie, who were still invisible. From the back of the van, they could hear every word.

The two children didn't know what to do. Why was the van in this dark garage? Who was the man at the computer, and how could he steal the van so easily?

Ben's first idea was just to wait. When nobody else was in the van, he could try and take the van home. But the man in glasses never left the front seat.

Other men were looking around the van. Suddenly one opened the back door. Was he going to find Ben and Rosie?

Quickly Ben took his sister's hand. Without a word, they moved out of the van before the man heard them.

→ Go to page 40 for activities.

Ben and Rosie followed one of the men out of the garage and up some stairs.

Soon they came to a dark room, where a big man was talking to a group of people.

'Perhaps now you understand,' Cooger said softly. 'With that van we'll steal more than anybody in history.'

The picture on the screen showed a room full of shelves. On each shelf there were lots of gold bars.

'This is the government's gold and it's in the country's safest bank,' said Cooger. 'Nobody has ever stolen any of it. Nobody has ever tried ... until today.'

Cooger stopped. He turned his head.
'Did you hear something?' he said.

The others listened for a moment.

'I didn't hear anything,' said one man.

'Nothing,' said another.

Cooger held up his hand. 'Be quiet,' he told them.
'I'm the greatest criminal in this city. I've never been
caught by the police, and I never will be caught. And
do you know why? Because I *always* know when
something is wrong.' He stood up slowly. 'And believe
me – something is wrong.'

→ Go to page 41 for activities.

Chapter Four

As Cooger stood up, Ben and Rosie looked at the open door. Should they try to run?

But it was too late. 'Close the door,' Cooger told one of his men.

Cooger began to walk around the room. Ben and Rosie tried not to move or make a sound.

'In a few minutes, the van will leave for the bank,' Cooger said. 'But we can't just sit here and wait … because we're not alone in this room.'

He picked something up from a table in the corner – a box of matches.

Cooger took out a match. He lit it and then held it up to the ceiling.

'What's he doing?' thought Ben.

A moment later he understood. This building had sprinklers to stop fires. As soon as the match came close to the ceiling, the sprinklers turned on. Water went everywhere.

'Why did you do that, Mr Cooger?' shouted one of the men. 'We're getting wet!'

But Cooger was pointing to two shapes which they could now see in the water.

Go to page 42 for activities.

'Get them!' shouted Cooger.

Rosie pulled her brother's hand. 'Run!'

But there was nowhere to run to ... until somebody opened the door. 'The van's ready to leave, Mr Cooger,' said Professor Sparrow.

'Close that door!' shouted Cooger angrily, but he was too late. Ben and Rosie moved fast and ran past the scientist.

They could hear Cooger's angry shout behind them: 'Don't let them leave the building!'

Outside the room, Rosie asked, 'Which way now?'

'To the stairs!' answered Ben.

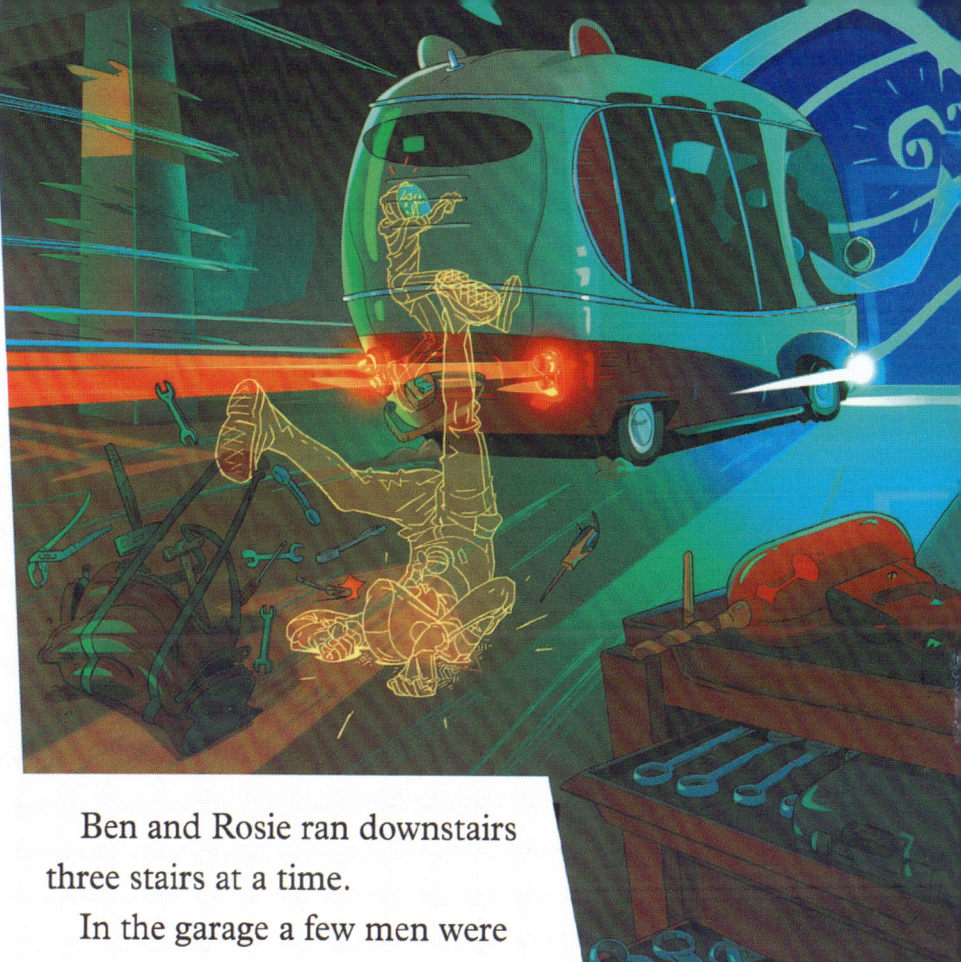

Ben and Rosie ran downstairs three stairs at a time.

In the garage a few men were already sitting in the van.

'Sparrow programmed the computer,' one of them said. 'Just hit the screen and the van will go.'

The van started.

'We can't let them use our van!' said Rosie. 'Come on!'

She pulled Ben's hand and ran.

Bright lights had appeared in front of the van – it was leaving. Rosie jumped. Ben jumped too, but his foot hit a bag on the floor and he fell. When he looked up, the van wasn't there.

→ Go to page 43 for activities.

Chapter Five

'Rosie?' whispered Ben. 'Are you still here?'

The person who answered wasn't Rosie.

'I was right,' said Cooger from the door behind Ben. 'Somebody *has* come into my building.' He was speaking quietly again. To Ben that soft voice was more frightening than any angry shout.

Ben looked up nervously. There were no sprinklers in this part of the building. 'He can't see me,' thought Ben. 'I'll be alright if I can just stay quiet.'

But Cooger didn't look worried. He closed the door and smiled. 'That's the only way out,' he said.

The criminal was holding something in one hand.

'I'm not a scientist,' he said in a relaxed, friendly voice. 'But I love science. I love new inventions! They're like toys for me.' He walked slowly around the room. 'Here's a fun "toy" that Sparrow made for me.'

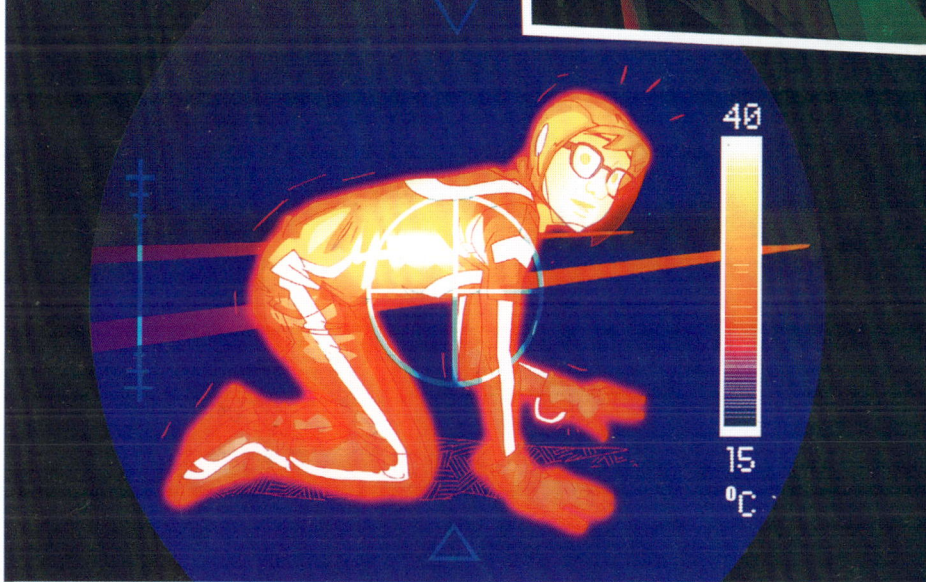

He held up the thing in his hand. 'These glasses let me see in the dark,' he said. 'They don't show light – they show *heat*.'

Cooger carefully put the glasses on, and then he smiled. 'That's better,' he said. 'Now I can see you.'

→ Go to page 44 for activities.

Ben knew that he didn't have to stay quiet anymore – Cooger could see him.

'Then watch this!' Ben shouted. He began to run to the other side of the room. Perhaps there was a window or door that Cooger had forgotten about.

When Cooger started to run too, Ben was surprised. Though he was a big man, the criminal moved fast – very fast.

Ben tried to change direction, but Cooger was too quick for him. Ben felt a hand on the material at the back of his neck.

As Ben tried to run away, Cooger's hand hit the button on the suit's sleeve. There was a click, and suddenly Ben wasn't invisible anymore.

Cooger took off his glasses and studied the suit. 'Amazing,' he said. 'Was this made by the same man who made the van?'

'I won't tell you anything,' said Ben.

Cooger smiled. 'So you won't tell me about your little friend? There were two of you upstairs, but now there's only one. I hope that he or she didn't leave with the van. Because that would be *very* dangerous.'

→ Go to page 45 for activities.

Chapter Six

Ben was sitting in a small room with no windows. Cooger had taken the invisibility suit from him and then brought him there.

But where was Rosie? Was she safe? Ben couldn't stop thinking about his sister. Cooger's words returned to his mind: '*very* dangerous.'

Ben looked up when the door started to open. Had Cooger come back to ask more questions?

No – the person at the door was Professor Sparrow. The scientist pushed his glasses up his nose and said, 'We don't have much time. Follow me.'

When they were outside the room, Ben asked, 'Why are you helping me?'

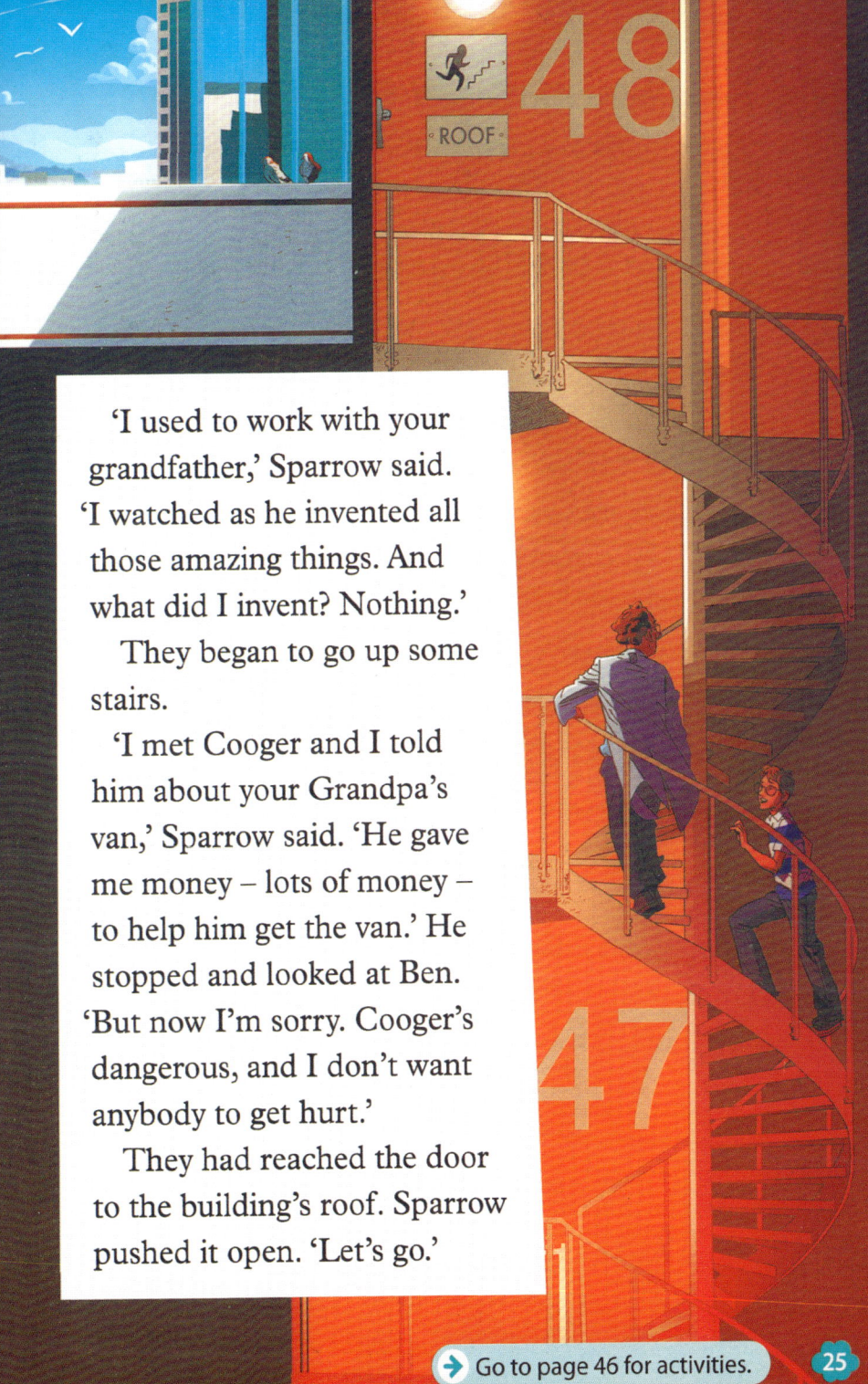

'I used to work with your grandfather,' Sparrow said. 'I watched as he invented all those amazing things. And what did I invent? Nothing.'

They began to go up some stairs.

'I met Cooger and I told him about your Grandpa's van,' Sparrow said. 'He gave me money – lots of money – to help him get the van.' He stopped and looked at Ben. 'But now I'm sorry. Cooger's dangerous, and I don't want anybody to get hurt.'

They had reached the door to the building's roof. Sparrow pushed it open. 'Let's go.'

→ Go to page 46 for activities.

Rosie was as frightened as her brother.

She had reached the back of the van before it left. Moments later it arrived in the bank room that Cooger had spoken about. Rosie had never seen so much gold.

'What's happening?' shouted a guard in surprise.

Cooger's men had put on gas masks. As soon as they jumped out of the van, one of the men opened something. Immediately there was gas everywhere. The guards fell to the floor and began to sleep.

'You'll wake up with a headache and a lot less gold!' laughed one of Cooger's men.

Rosie held one hand over her mouth. Then she saw a gas mask in the van. She picked it up and held it over her mouth.

Cooger's men were too busy to see this. They were carrying heavy gold bars to the back of the van.

Quickly, Rosie ran to the driver's seat. She started to type the computer code so that she could drive the van with her voice.

At last one of Cooger's men saw Rosie's mask. 'What's *that*?' he shouted.

→ Go to page 47 for activities.

Chapter Seven

One of Cooger's men ran to the front of the van, but Rosie had finished the code. She pulled the hood of the invisibility suit down, so the man could see her face.

'Who are you?' he asked from behind his gas mask.

'I'm the girl who's going to stop you,' said Rosie. 'Van, take us out of here!'

The man tried to reach into the van to turn it off, but he didn't have enough time. His hand closed on air, and nothing else.

At Cooger's building, Sparrow and Ben ran onto the roof.

Cooger was waiting with two of his men. 'I'm disappointed in you, Professor Sparrow,' he said sadly. 'And when I'm disappointed, I get very angry.' He moved closer to the scientist.

'I've already called the police,' said Sparrow. 'They'll be here soon.'

Cooger just laughed. 'The police can't catch me!' He held up the invisibility suit. 'I have *this*! It's as useful as the van. I can use it to go in and out of any bank in the world.'

→ Go to page 48 for activities.

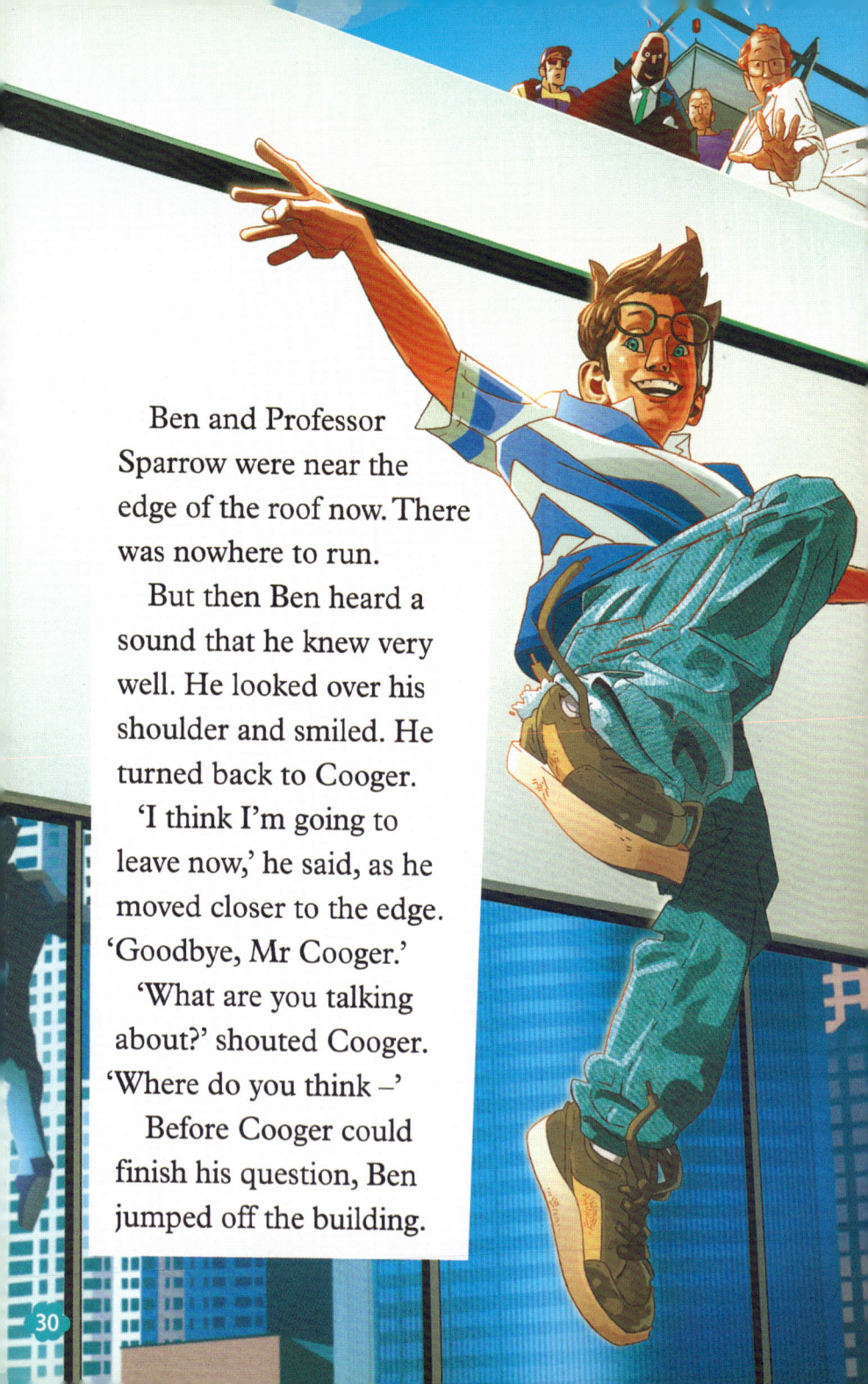

Ben and Professor Sparrow were near the edge of the roof now. There was nowhere to run.

But then Ben heard a sound that he knew very well. He looked over his shoulder and smiled. He turned back to Cooger.

'I think I'm going to leave now,' he said, as he moved closer to the edge. 'Goodbye, Mr Cooger.'

'What are you talking about?' shouted Cooger. 'Where do you think –'

Before Cooger could finish his question, Ben jumped off the building.

'No!' shouted Sparrow.

A moment later the van slowly moved up until Cooger could see it. Ben was sitting happily on the van's roof. His sister was in the driver's seat. They both smiled at Cooger.

'Perhaps you didn't know that the van could fly, too?' shouted Rosie.

Ben looked at Professor Sparrow. 'Come with us,' he said.

The scientist pushed his glasses up his nose. 'Thank you, but no,' he answered. 'I did something that was very wrong. But now I'm going to do the right thing.'

Rosie understood. 'Van, take us home,' she said.

Go to page 49 for activities.

Chapter Eight

When the van arrived home, Grandpa was waiting with Alice and Max.

'We've been so worried!' said Alice. 'Where were you?'

'It's a long story,' said Ben. He and Rosie began to tell them about their adventure. When they had finished, Max looked in the back of the van.

'There's still lots of gold here,' he said, amazed. 'But how can we return it to the bank? The police will think that *we* stole it.'

'Don't worry,' said Grandpa. 'I know a police officer who I can talk to. Giving the gold back won't be a problem.'

Ben looked unhappy.

'What's wrong?' asked Alice.

'Well, the police are going to catch all of Cooger's men, but they won't catch Cooger,' he said. 'He's got the invisibility suit. He can just put it on and walk past the police without a problem.'

'That's not really true, Ben,' Grandpa said. 'The suits can only stay invisible for a short time. For Mr Cooger's suit, that time will end ...' He looked at his watch. 'Now!'

→ Go to page 50 for activities.

Outside Cooger's building there were lots of police officers. They'd waited a long, long time to catch Cooger's men. Now they had caught almost all of them.

'But where's Cooger?' one police officer asked. 'He's the one who makes all the plans.'

The police officer didn't know it, but at that moment Cooger walked past her. With the invisibility suit on, the criminal thought that he was safe. He didn't have to hurry.

Cooger tried hard not to laugh. 'They'll never catch me,' he thought happily.

Cooger didn't know that a police officer was pointing at him. The criminal didn't know that the invisibility suit had stopped working. He was trying to leave in a suit that was as yellow as a banana!

'Who's that?' someone asked.

Sparrow was getting into the back of a police car. 'That's the man you're looking for,' he said happily.

When Cooger looked around again, every police officer was looking at him. Some were laughing. Cooger tried to run, but there were police officers everywhere.

Sparrow watched as Cooger was taken to a different police car. The scientist pushed his glasses higher and laughed.

Go to page 51 for activities.

Activities for pages 4–5

1 **Choose and write the correct words.**

> a projector   ~~a scientist~~   silent   nervous   to disappear

1 This is a person who studies the world.   _a scientist_

2 When something suddenly can't be seen.   _____

3 This means the same as quiet.   _____

4 This can be connected to a computer to make the pictures on the screen much bigger.   _____

5 This means the same as worried.   _____

2 **Write *yes* or *no*.**

1 Professor Sparrow is a scientist.   _yes_

2 When he walked into the dark room, Sparrow felt happy.   _____

3 Lots of men were looking at Sparrow.   _____

4 Cooger wanted Sparrow to make them all famous.   _____

5 Sparrow showed the men an amazing van on a screen.   _____

6 The van could go anywhere in the world very quickly.   _____

Talk **Who do you think made the amazing van? Tell a friend your ideas.**

Activities for pages 6–7

1 **Read the sentences. Choose and write the correct words.**

1 Grandpa is the smartest person Sparrow ___has___ ever met.

   a has **b** is **c** does

2 Rosie couldn't _____ Grandpa in the backyard.

   a seen **b** saw **c** see

3 At first Rosie could _____ see Grandpa's head.

   a either **b** yet **c** only

4 Grandpa was _____ a yellow suit.

   a wearing **b** wear **c** worn

5 Grandpa was testing _____ new invention.

   a he's **b** his **c** him

2 **Circle the correct words.**

1 **Everybody / Nobody** was laughing at Sparrow now.

2 **Grandpa / Sparrow** made the amazing van.

3 When Rosie got to the backyard, it was **empty / busy**.

4 Suddenly Rosie **saw / heard** Grandpa's voice.

5 Then Rosie saw Grandpa's head **appear / disappear**.

6 Rosie **dropped / ate** the cookies.

7 Rosie heard a click, and saw **all / some** of Grandpa.

1 Choose and write the correct words.

Grandpa told Ben and Rosie ¹___about___ his new invention.

His invention was a ²_____ suit. It was a new kind

³_____ material. Light ⁴_____ in straight

lines, but it travels around the new material. This means

the suit, and anyone ⁵_____ the suit, is invisible.

Grandpa wanted to use the suit to ⁶_____ birds in the

backyard. Ben and Rosie's ⁷_____ were coming for

a trip in the van. Grandpa ⁸_____ Ben and Rosie to

meet him at the van ⁹_____ ten minutes.

1 **a** for **b** ~~about~~ **c** around **d** at

2 **a** specially **b** especially **c** special **d** specials

3 **a** for **b** to **c** at **d** of

4 **a** travelled **b** travel **c** travelling **d** travels

5 **a** outside **b** near **c** in **d** on

6 **a** watching **b** watch **c** watched **d** watches

7 **a** family **b** brothers **c** friends **d** sisters

8 **a** said **b** told **c** shouted **d** called

9 **a** on **b** at **c** for **d** in

1 Order the words.

1 put on / Ben / yellow / and Rosie / suits. / the

   Ben and Rosie put on the yellow suits.

2 pushed / disappeared. / Ben / a button / immediately / and

   _____

3 in / Ben / the back / the van. / and Rosie / of / hid

   _____

4 got / the van. / Two / men / into

   _____

5 the van / move. / Suddenly / started / to

   _____

2 Circle the mistakes. Then write the correct words.

1 Ben and Rosie played with the (van.)   *suits*

2 Then Ben had an idea.   _____

3 Ben and Rosie wanted to frighten Alice
   and Max.   _____

4 Then a man opened the van window.   _____

5 Ben knew the men might be friendly.   _____

6 Ben and Rosie wanted to leave through
   the front door.   _____

Talk **Who are the men? Tell a friend your ideas.**

1 Complete the sentences.

> door   garage   idea   van   ~~building~~   problem

1 Sparrow wanted to take the van to Cooger's ___building___ .

2 He took the van to the _____ under the building.

3 Sparrow was surprised there wasn't a _____ .

4 At first, Ben's _____ was to wait.

5 Someone opened the back _____ of the van.

6 Quickly Ben and Rosie got out of the _____ .

2 Circle the correct answers.

1 Who got into the van?

> Grandpa   (Sparrow)   Cooger

2 Why didn't Sparrow see Ben and Rosie?

> they were quiet   they got out   they were invisible

3 What did Ben want to wait for?

> Grandpa to come   the men to leave
> the van to disappear

4 Did Sparrow get out of the van?

> yes   no   don't know

5 Did the man find Ben and Rosie?

> yes   no   don't know

1 Choose the correct answers.

1 Who was Cooger talking to?

   a A group of police officers.

   b A group of scientists.

   c A group of frightened men.

   d A group of criminals.

2 Why did Cooger and his men steal Grandpa's van?

   a They wanted to steal money from the government.

   b They wanted to be the greatest criminals in the city.

   c They wanted to steal gold from the government.

   d They wanted to be better than anyone in history.

3 What did Cooger say about himself?

   a He'll never know when something is wrong.

   b He'll never be caught by the police.

   c He'll be the greatest criminal in the city.

   d He'll try something many people have tried.

4 Why did Cooger think something was wrong?

   a He heard something.

   b He saw something on the screen.

   c He always knows when something is wrong.

   d The men said they heard something.

1 Find and write the words.

1 This means the same as noise.   s o u n d

2 This is when you are on your own.   a _ _ _ _

3 You can use this to make fire.   m _ _ _ _

4 This is the very top of a room.   c _ _ _ _ _ _

5 Water comes out of this to
   put out a fire.   s _ _ _ _ _ _ _ _

6 A square and a circle are these.   s _ _ _ _ _

2 Look at the picture at the bottom of page 17 and write *yes* or *no*.

1 Cooger's mouth is open.   yes

2 Cooger is wearing a green jacket.   _____

3 Water is falling on to Cooger's head.   _____

4 Cooger is pointing at Ben and Rosie.   _____

5 There is a door behind Ben and Rosie.   _____

6 There is a man waiting at the door.   _____

7 Cooger has a cell phone in his pocket.   _____

8 Cooger has brown hair.   _____

Talk **Why did Cooger make the sprinklers come on?
Talk to a friend.**

Activities for pages 18–19

1 **Decide if the sentences are *correct* (A) or *incorrect* (B).**

  1 Cooger could see Ben and Rosie.   (A) B

  2 Cooger wanted the men to catch Ben and Rosie.   A B

  3 Ben opened the door to the room.   A B

  4 Ben and Rosie ran out of the room.   A B

  5 Ben and Rosie ran to the top of the building.   A B

  6 Some men were sitting in the van.   A B

  7 Sparrow was in the van programming
the computer.   A B

  8 A man hit the screen and the van started.   A B

  9 Ben and Rosie jumped into the van.   A B

 10 The van disappeared.   A B

2 **Look at pages 18 and 19 and complete the sentences. You can use 1, 2, 3, or 4 words.**

  1 There was nowhere to run until <u>somebody opened the</u> door.

  2 The van was _____ to leave.

  3 Ben and Rosie ran _____ scientist.

  4 In the garage a few _____ in the van.

  5 One man hit the screen and _____ started.

Talk **Where is the van going? Tell a friend your ideas.**

Activities for pages 20–21

1 Order the words.

1 was / Cooger. / still in / Ben / the building / with

_____

2 knew / his building. / Cooger / was in / someone

_____

3 nervously. / up / Ben / looked

_____

4 had / in / Cooger / his hand. / some glasses

_____

5 see in / let / The glasses / the dark. / Cooger

_____

6 show / The / heat, / glasses / not light.

_____

2 Circle the correct words.

1 The person **what** / **who** answered Ben wasn't Rosie.

2 Cooger was speaking in a **soft** / **softly** voice.

3 Cooger closed the door and **smiled** / **smiles**.

4 Cooger loves science and **newer** / **new** inventions.

5 Cooger's glasses show **hot** / **heat**.

6 Sparrow **made** / **was making** the glasses for Cooger.

7 Cooger put the glasses **up** / **on**.

8 Now he could **see** / **saw** Ben.

✿ **Activities** for pages 22–23

1 Choose and write the correct words.

Now Cooger ¹_____ see Ben. Ben tried to run
²_____ and find a window or door Cooger had
³_____ about. But Cooger was very ⁴_____. Ben
felt a hand on ⁵_____ back of his suit. Then Cooger's
hand hit the ⁶_____ on the sleeve and suddenly Ben
⁷_____ invisible. Cooger asked Ben ⁸_____
made the suit. Ben didn't tell ⁹_____. Cooger said it
was ¹⁰_____ for Rosie to be in the van.

1 **a** should **b** might **c** could **d** ought to

2 **a** away **b** up **c** over **d** out

3 **a** forgot **b** forget **c** forgetting **d** forgotten

4 **a** faster **b** fastest **c** fasting **d** fast

5 **a** at **b** that **c** the **d** a

6 **a** button **b** computer **c** match **d** screen

7 **a** couldn't **b** hadn't **c** didn't **d** wasn't

8 **a** what **b** where **c** which **d** who

9 **a** it **b** him **c** his **d** that

10 **a** danger **b** dangerously **c** dangerous **d** in danger

Activities for pages 24–25

1 Order the events.

Ben followed Professor Sparrow. _____

Ben and Sparrow went up some stairs. _____

Ben was sitting in a small room. __1__

Sparrow opened the door onto the roof. _____

Professor Sparrow opened the door to the small room. _____

Sparrow said he was sorry for helping Cooger. _____

Cooger told Ben that he used to work with Grandpa. _____

2 Match. Then write the sentences.

Cooger had taken • • about Rosie.

Ben was worried • • went to the roof.

Professor Sparrow used • • about Grandpa's van.

Sparrow told Cooger • • was sorry.

But now Sparrow • • Ben's invisibility suit.

Sparrow and Ben • • to work with Grandpa.

1 Cooger had taken Ben's invisibility suit.

2 _____

3 _____

4 _____

5 _____

6 _____

1 Circle the mistakes. Then write the correct words.

1 Rosie was as frightened to Ben.   _____

2 The van arrived on the bank room.   _____

3 Rosie had never seen so many gold.   _____

4 The men had put out gas masks.   _____

5 Rosie saw a gas mask and pick it up.   _____

6 Cooger's men were to busy to see Rosie.   _____

2 Circle the correct answers.

1 Where did the van go?

   to the garage   to the bank   to Grandpa's house

2 What made the guards go to sleep?

   a man hit him   the van   gas

3 What did Rosie hold over her mouth?

   her sleeve   a gas mask   some gold

4 What could Rosie drive the van with?

   her hands   her suit   her voice

5 What did one of the men see?

   Rosie's mask   Rosie   Rosie's suit

Talk **Can Rosie get away from Cooger's men? Tell a friend your ideas.**

Activities for pages 28–29

1 **Choose the correct answers.**

1 Why did Rosie show the man her face?

   a She wanted to frighten him.

   b She wanted time to type in the computer code.

   c She knew she could get away.

   d She wanted the man to help her.

2 What happened when the man tried to turn off the van?

   a He was too late and the van had gone.

   b He had just enough time.

   c He could see Rosie's face.

   d The van took him with Rosie.

3 What happened when Ben and Sparrow got to the roof?

   a Cooger called the police.

   b Cooger was very disappointed in Ben.

   c Cooger was waiting for them.

   d Cooger moved closer to two of his men.

4 Why did Cooger just laugh?

   a Because he gets angry when he's disappointed.

   b Because the police were coming.

   c Because Ben and Sparrow were on the roof.

   d Because he had the invisibility suit.

1 Read the sentences. Choose and write the correct words.

1 Ben was _____ the edge of the roof.

  a next **b** near **c** about

2 Ben moved _____ to the edge.

  a closer **b** closest **c** closely

3 Then Ben jumped _____ the building.

  a up **b** out **c** off

4 Ben _____ on the roof of the van.

  a land **b** landed **c** landing

5 Cooger didn't know the van _____ fly.

  a could **b** might **c** must

6 Professor Sparrow didn't go _____ the children.

  a for **b** along **c** with

2 Match.

1 Ben heard a	onto the van's roof.
2 The sound was	the driver's seat.
3 Ben jumped	sound that he knew well.
4 Rosie was in	smiled at Cooger.
5 Ben and Rosie	Grandpa's van.

1 **Circle the correct words.**

1 **At** / **In** home, Grandpa, Alice, and Max were waiting.

2 Rosie and Ben began to **told** / **tell** their story.

3 There was **still** / **yet** lots of gold in the back of the van.

4 Giving the gold back **couldn't** / **wouldn't** be a problem.

5 Ben was unhappy that Cooger **had** / **have** the invisibility suit.

6 Cooger could **wear** / **put** the suit on and walk past the police.

7 The suits stay invisible **since** / **for** a short time.

2 **Who said this? Write the names.**

1 'I have important friends in the police.'   _Grandpa_

2 'We've been so worried!'   _____

3 'The suits can only stay invisible for a short time.'   _____

4 'There's still lots of gold here.'   _____

5 'What's wrong?'   _____

6 'He's got the invisibility suit.'   _____

7 'The police will think that *we* stole it.'   _____

8 'It's a long story.'   _____

Talk **What happens to Cooger? Tell a friend your ideas.**

1 Decide if the sentences are *correct* (A) or *incorrect* (B).

1 There were lots of police officers outside Cooger's building. **A   B**

2 The police officers had wanted to catch Cooger for a long time. **A   B**

3 Cooger's men made all the plans. **A   B**

4 Cooger thought he was safe in the suit. **A   B**

5 When he walked past the police officers, Cooger didn't hurry. **A   B**

6 The police officers could suddenly see Cooger. **A   B**

7 Cooger had taken the invisibility suit off. **A   B**

8 Sparrow told the police officers it was Cooger. **A   B**

9 The police officers let Sparrow go. **A   B**

10 Cooger was put into a police car. **A   B**

2 Order the events.

Sparrow got into a police car. _____

Cooger walked past a police officer. _____

Lots of police officers were waiting for Cooger. _____

Cooger was taken to a police car. _____

A police officer pointed at Cooger. _____

Talk **Do you like this story? Talk to a friend.**

An Invisibility Story

1 Imagine you had an invisibility suit like Grandpa's for one day. Where would you go and what would you do? Make some notes.

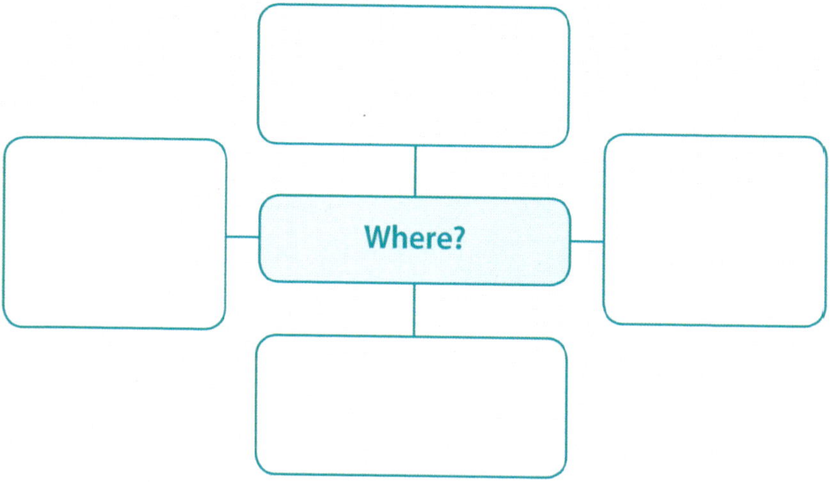

Where?

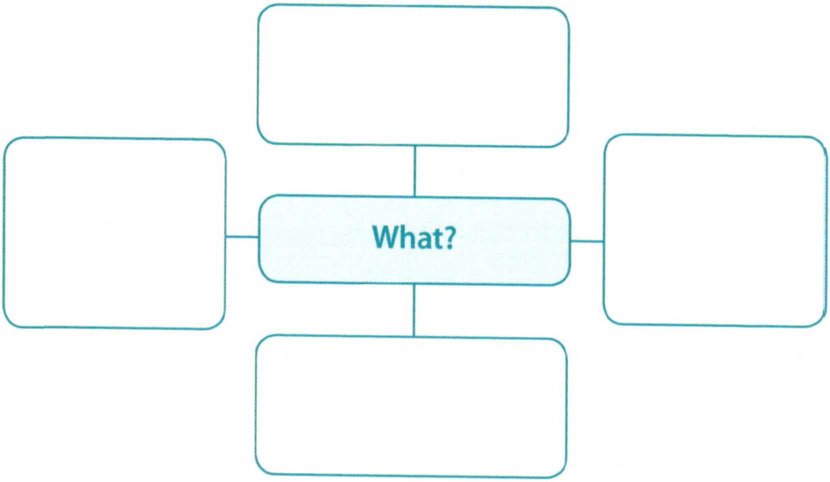

What?

Talk Compare your notes with a friend's notes. Are they similar or different?

2 You are going to write a story based on your notes. First write a short plan of your story.

Where –

When –

Characters (people) –

Plot (what happens) –

Ending –

3 Now write your story.

Talk Read your story to a friend. Now listen to their story.

Glossary

Here are some words used in this book, and you can check what they mean. Use a dictionary to check other new words.

anywhere *adverb*
in, at, or to any place

appear *verb*
to suddenly be seen

bar *noun*
a small piece of something hard

catch *verb*
to find and hold someone or something

click *noun*
a short, sharp sound

code *noun*
a group of numbers or letters that helps you find something

cold *adjective*
not friendly or kind

connected *adjective*
(of two or more things or people) having a link between them

cookie *noun*
a kind of cake that is small, thin, and sweet

cool *adjective*
People say 'Cool!' to show that they think something is a good idea.

criminal *noun*
a person who does something that is against the law

disappear *verb*
If a person or thing disappears, they go away so people cannot see them.

edge *noun*
the part along the side or the end of something

everywhere *adverb*
in all places or to all places

fashion *noun*
a way of dressing or doing something that people like and try to copy for a time

fashionable *adjective*
popular, or in a popular style

follow *verb*
to come or go after someone or something

forget *verb*
to not remember something

garage *noun*
a building where you keep a car

gas *noun*
something like air

give someone back something
to return something to someone

gold *noun*
a yellow metal that is very expensive

headache *noun*
a pain in your head

heat *noun*
something that is hot has a lot of heat

hood *noun*
the part of a jacket or sweater that covers your head and neck

hurry *verb*
to move or do something quickly

imagine *verb*
to make a picture of something in your mind

invention *noun*
a thing that someone has made for the first time

invisible *adjective*
If something is invisible, you cannot see it.

light *noun*
the energy from the sun, a lamp, etc. that allows us to see things

mask *noun*
a thing that you wear over your face to hide or protect it

match *noun*
a short thin piece of wood that you use to light a fire

material *noun*
cloth that you use for making clothes and other things

nothing *pronoun*
not anything; no thing

nowhere *adverb*
not anywhere; at, in, or to no place

program *verb*
to give a set of instructions to a computer

projector *noun*
a machine that shows movies or pictures on a wall or screen

return *verb*
to give, put, send, or take something back

right *adjective*
good; the opposite of wrong

roof *noun*
the top of a building or car

shape *noun*
what you see if you draw a line around something

show *verb*
to let someone see something; to appear or be seen

silently *adverb*
without speaking; without making any or much sound

sleeve *noun*
the part of a coat, dress, shirt, etc. that covers your arm

smart *adjective*
able to learn and think quickly; intelligent

someone *pronoun*
a person; a person that you do not know

sprinkler *noun*
a thing that sends out water in small drops. Sprinklers are used on grass and for stopping fires in buildings.

straight *adjective*
going in one direction only

suit *noun*
a jacket and pants, or a jacket and skirt, that you wear together and that are made from the same material

test *verb*
to use or look at something carefully to find out how good it is or if it works well

voice *noun*
the sounds that you make when you speak or sing

whisper *verb*
to speak very quietly to someone, so that other people cannot hear what you are saying

wrong *adjective*
bad, or not what the law allows

yard *noun*
an area next to a building or house, sometimes with grass and trees in it and a wall around it

Definitions in this glossary are taken and adapted from
Oxford American Dictionaries for learners of English

Oxford Read and Imagine

Oxford Read and Imagine graded readers are at nine levels (Early Starter, Starter, Beginner, and Levels 1 to 6) for students from age 3 or 4 and older. They offer great stories to read and enjoy.

Activities provide Cambridge Young Learners Exams preparation. See Key below.

At Levels 1 to 6, every storybook reader links to an **Oxford Read and Discover** non-fiction reader, giving students a chance to find out more about the world around them, and an opportunity for Content and Language Integrated Learning (CLIL).

For more information about **Read and Imagine**, and for Teacher's Notes, go to www.oup.com/elt/teacher/readandimagine

KEY
KET Activity supports Cambridge Key English Test Exam preparation
PET Activity supports Cambridge Preliminary English Test Exam preparation

 Oxford Read and Discover

Invisible! is a story about what clothes could be like in the future. To find out about fabrics, clothes and fashion, you can read this non-fiction book.

Clothes Then and Now

OXFORD
UNIVERSITY PRESS

Great Clarendon Street, Oxford, OX2 6DP, United Kingdom

Oxford University Press is a department of the University of Oxford. It furthers the University's objective of excellence in research, scholarship, and education by publishing worldwide. Oxford is a registered trade mark of Oxford University Press in the UK and in certain other countries

ISBN: 978 0 19 472384 8

Printed in China

This book is printed on paper from certified and well-managed sources

ACKNOWLEDGEMENTS
Main illustrations by: Carl Pearce/Advocate Art